21st CENTURY CITIZEN

Immigrants and Refugees

Cath Senker

FRANKLIN WATTS

Titles in this series:
AIDS
Animal Rights
Genetic Engineering
Immigrants and Refugees
Terrorism
World Hunger

© 2004 Arcturus Publishing Ltd

Produced for Franklin Watts by
Arcturus Publishing Ltd, 26/27 Bickels Yard,
151-153 Bermondsey Street, London SE1 3HA.

Series concept: Alex Woolf
Editor: Kelly Davis
Designer: Stonecastle Graphics
Consultant: Kaye Stearman
Picture researcher: Shelley Noronha,
    Glass Onion Pictures

Published in the UK by Franklin Watts.

British Library Cataloguing Publication Data
A CIP catalogue record for this book is
available from the British Library.

ISBN 0 7496 5464 3

Printed and bound in Italy

Franklin Watts – the Watts Publishing Group,
96 Leonard Street, London EC2A 4XD.

Picture acknowledgements
Exile Images 7 (N. Cooper), 43 (H. Davies); Eye
Ubiquitous 41 (Matthew Mckee); Impact 20
(Chris Moyse); Panos Pictures 37 (Chris
Stowers); Photri 21 (Jeff Greenberg); Popperfoto
1 and 28, 9, 11, 12, 14, 15, 26; Rex Features 4
(Roger Viollet), 30, 33 (Jenny Matthews), 34, 35,
36; Topham 6 (Sonda Dawes), 8, 10, 16, 17, 18
(David Wells), 19 and 22 (Rob Crandall), 24, 27
and cover, below, 31, 38, 39, 42, 44 and cover,
above (Michael Schwartz).

**Cover pictures: People being sworn in as US citizens in
Atlanta, Georgia, USA (above). An Iraqi refugee with
his three-year-old daughter at a French refugee camp
(below).**

Note to parents and teachers
Some recommended websites are listed under
'Useful Addresses' at the back of this book.
Every effort has been made by the Publishers to
ensure that these websites are suitable for
children; that they are of the highest
educational value; and that they contain no
inappropriate or offensive material. However,
because of the nature of the Internet, it is
impossible to guarantee that the contents of
these sites will not be altered. We strongly
advise that Internet access is supervised by a
responsible adult.

Acknowledgements
The author would like to thank the following
for permission to reproduce material for case
studies from their publications: MacRoberts
Arts Centre, *Club Asylum* 7; Leverton and
Lowensohn, *I Came Alone* 15; Ghada Karmi, *In
Search of Fatima* 16; Save the Children Fund,
Separated Children Coming to Western Europe 30;
Index on Censorship, *Double Crossings* 34;
Nicole Constable, *Guardian* story from *Maid to
Order in Hong Kong: Stories of Filipina Workers* 35.

Contents

1: Who are Immigrants and Refugees?

Where are you from? Perhaps you were born in a different country from the one you live in now. Or maybe you have always lived there. But where are your parents and grandparents from? Maybe your family originally came from a different country. I live in England. One hundred years ago, my Jewish great-grandparents escaped persecution in Poland, Russia and Romania and came to Britain for a better life. My great-

In the late nineteenth and twentieth centuries, many eastern European Jews, like these immigrants at a New York street market in 1914, made their way to the USA for a better life.

PERSPECTIVES

'International migration … has always existed. Twice as many people migrated from Europe as have come in the opposite direction. And since the current theory is that human beings originated in East Africa, every other part of the world is the product of immigration. All of us … are either immigrants or descended from immigrants.'

Teresa Hayter, author on immigration issues, 2002

grandfather aimed to go to Leeds in the north of England. But he couldn't pronounce it properly and he ended up in Leith in Scotland instead! Some members of the extended family went to the USA.

People who have come to a country to settle permanently are known as immigrants. If they intend to leave a country permanently, they are usually called emigrants. Anyone who moves is a migrant. And those who move for a better life are often called economic migrants.

It is estimated that around 7 per cent of the world's population were born in another country from the one they live in. About 3 per cent migrated openly (legally) and around 4 per cent are undocumented (illegal) immigrants. Faster and cheaper transport, and good communications, have made it easier to move from country to country.

Types of immigrants

Legal immigrants are people who have sought permission to enter a new country to live. They often have skills to offer and may have relatives already living in the country. For example, a professional family may move from China to Canada to enjoy better living standards.

There are also undocumented immigrants, who have moved to a country illegally. Perhaps they have overstayed a tourist visa or been smuggled in. In the USA, for example, there are millions of Latin Americans who have entered the country without permission and are picking fruit in the fields or cleaning offices across the land. Finally, there are people who are forced to migrate. Traffickers may force the unsuspecting to move abroad to do unpleasant jobs (see page 34).

Who is a refugee?

Refugees are people who flee their country to escape from war or persecution. Usually, they want to go home once their country is safe again. About 15 million people worldwide are refugees, and around 22 million others are displaced – forced to move within their own country. Over half of all the world's refugees are children.

Which of the following do you think would count as refugees? During the 1980s and 1990s, three million Afghans fled to Pakistan for safety due to civil war. Kambar was among them. In 1990s Iraq, Amira feared imprisonment and torture for opposing Saddam Hussein's brutal regime. She escaped to the USA. And Atak, of the Dinka people, was forced to leave his home in Sudan and go elsewhere in the country, because his village was attacked during the civil war in the 1980s. He has not been able to return since.

The 1951 Convention on the Status of Refugees states that refugees are people who leave their country due to persecution for 'reasons of race, religion, nationality, social group or political opinion'. According to this definition, both Kambar and Amira are refugees. When refugees arrive in a country and apply for asylum – to stay there in safety – they are called asylum seekers. However, Atak is an Internally Displaced Person. Since he has not crossed an international border, he is not counted as a refugee.

Refugees and immigrants are not the same, but they may have similar reasons for leaving their own countries. For example, a Colombian may move to the USA not only because wages are higher but also because of political unrest in his or her own

A Hispanic worker picks tomatoes in Virginia, USA. The tomato harvest provides employment for thousands of seasonal workers, many of whom are from Latin American countries.

PERSPECTIVES

'When I was eight my parents got divorced and we were short of money. Mum sold some pictures she'd painted and went to live and work in Laredo [USA]. She didn't know anyone there. We lived on the Mexican side of the border, in Nuevo Laredo.'

Leticia, a Mexican woman, Mexican Migration Project

CASE STUDY

Mrs J comes from Somalia. When civil war broke out in 1999 her life suddenly changed:

'Before the war, we lived in a peaceful, friendly community. Then the war started. You couldn't trust your neighbours any more. People were being cut and burned and I decided to leave. My two daughters, two sons and I travelled by boat to Kenya. The boat was crowded and people were being thrown off into the water. We had no food, just water. In Kenya we spent three weeks locked in a garage with 200 other people. We paid someone over $5,000 [£3,000] to get us on a plane in Nairobi. We had no idea where we were going. We ended up in London, and later were sent to Glasgow in Scotland.'

(Source: Club Asylum, MacRobert Arts Centre, University of Stirling, Scotland)

country. This book will look at both immigrants and refugees, including the movement of people in history, their experiences and the impact they have on their new countries and those they leave behind. It will consider why immigration is such a controversial issue today and what can be done to build a more tolerant, accepting society.

What is the fuss about?

In many countries, increasing numbers of people see immigrants and refugees as a problem. There are fears that too many newcomers are arriving and stretching precious resources. Governments have policies to limit numbers of immigrants and refugees. These vary from country to country, and from year to year, depending on economic, humanitarian and social factors. In 1976, only 7 per cent of countries of the United Nations had policies aimed at restricting immigration. In 2000, 40 per cent did.

Yet the figures show that developed countries, like the UK and the USA, are not in fact being 'swamped by foreigners'. The proportions

A Sudanese woman boils leaves for her family to eat, south Sudan, 1999. The people shown here have been displaced from their homes by civil war and famine.

are actually quite small. For example, about 800,000 people enter the USA officially each year. This is well below the levels of official immigration in the early twentieth century. Around 10 per cent of the US population were born in another country. In the UK, about 4 per cent of the population are foreign-born. The flow of migration goes both ways – out of countries as well as into them. For example, in 2001, about 26,300 people came to live in Ireland (excluding asylum seekers), while 19,900 emigrated. Many people's fear of foreigners is actually due to racism. They do not want immigrants and refugees to come because many of them are black.

November 1992: a ship carrying Somali refugees finally enters Aden harbour in Yemen, after nine days at sea with no provisions. Somalia remains an unstable country today; in 2002 there were about 300,000 Somali refugees worldwide.

PERSPECTIVES

'The schools that have welcomed refugees have provided their American students with a gift like no other. Refugees offer students an opportunity to learn about world culture in a far more meaningful way than any textbook or filmstrip can provide. Refugees teach our children about compassion. They reinforce attributes of resilience and determination.'

Joyce L. Carroll, writing about Somali Bantu resettlement in the greater Burlington area in Burlington Free Press, *29 June 2003*

PERSPECTIVES

'A multicultural society ... has actually turned out to be a society with no culture at all, in which British history, traditions, customs and literature have been deliberately forgotten and even suppressed... Continued uncontrolled immigration from cultures quite different from our own will accelerate this process.'

Peter Hitchens, writing in the Mail on Sunday, *a British tabloid newspaper, quoted in* Double Crossings: Migration Now, *published by Index on Censorship, 2003*

A sense of panic

It is commonly believed in developed countries that there are so many asylum seekers that governments cannot cope with them. Again, the numbers are often not as great as people think. In Canada, for example, it is generally thought that the country takes more than its fair share of asylum seekers. But the number accepted each year is less than a tenth of 1 per cent of the population!

In developing countries, where 80 per cent of the world's refugees live, they have sometimes been welcomed. But not always. In poor countries nowadays, refugees can boost the economy but can also stretch already scarce resources.

The tightening up of immigration controls around the world indicates a sense of panic about migration. Yet evidence shows that immigrants bring skills and resources to their new country, and enrich its culture. And if we look at history, we can see that people have always moved from country to country.

Members of a far-right group demonstrate their hostility to undocumented immigrants (they call them 'illegals') in North Carolina, USA, 2000.

DEBATE

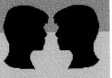

Why has the issue of immigrants and refugees become so important in your country?

2: A History of Movement

For as long as human beings have existed, they have moved around to find food, or to escape natural disasters or hostile neighbours. Before 1500 AD, most people moved to find better land. They often invaded and fought other groups to take over their territory. Then, generally, they mixed with the local population.

Between 1500 and 1800, there were enormous movements of people. Advances in sailing and navigation made it easier to travel large distances by sea. Europeans, in particular, travelled far and wide to trade, and to take control of other parts of the world. This was the beginning of modern colonialism. For example, colonists took over the Caribbean, and North, Central and South America. They seized Africans as slaves to work for them there. Between 1500 and 1870, around 12 million Africans were captured and enslaved. This was one of the biggest forced migrations ever known.

Slaves on a farm in Cumberland, USA, 1862. Today, 13 per cent of the US population is African-American.

PERSPECTIVES

'Over a million and a half captives died during the "Middle Passage" [the sea journey] between Africa and the New World; an unknown, but large, number died prior to embarkation [getting on the ships]; and once in the New World, between a tenth and a fifth of the slaves died within a year … In most parts of the Americas overwork, malnutrition and disease took a grim toll.'

Robin Blackburn, *author of* The Making of New World Slavery, *1997*

Paying their way

Hundreds of thousands of people migrated for many other reasons. For instance, convicts were sent to Australia from Europe, rather than being kept in prison at home. Other migrants from Europe were people with different religious beliefs from the majority, such as the Puritans and the Quakers, who moved to North America. And more than 30 per cent of all European migrants before 1800 moved as indentured labourers. This meant that they had to work for an employer for a certain number of years in order to pay for their passage there.

The second big period of international migration began in the early nineteenth century, and took place on a huge scale between 1850 and 1950. These were mostly Europeans – free labourers seeking new opportunities in another continent. From 1800 to 1925, between 50 and 60 million people left Europe, and 85 per cent of them settled in Australia, Canada, New Zealand, the USA and Argentina. These countries were dramatically changed by European settlement.

Young post-war immigrants at Ellis Island, off New York. The number of immigrants wanting to enter the USA increased dramatically during the 1930s and 1940s. By 1947, when this picture was taken, around 20 million immigrants had passed through the Ellis Island immigration reception centre.

After the First World War, restrictions were placed on the number of immigrants permitted to go to key destinations such as the USA and Canada. The Great Depression of the 1930s and then the disaster of the Second World War destroyed many Europeans' dreams of a better life across the Atlantic. Instead it was a period of forced removals of refugees (see pages 14-16).

Post-war migration

Maybe your family migrated after the Second World War to the country you live in now – or perhaps you know others who did? The war shook up lives for millions of people and many found themselves on the move.

Global migration changed after the Second World War. People from many more nations were moving and settling elsewhere. Large numbers migrated from Europe to Australia, for example. However, it was no longer mainly Europeans who moved. From the 1950s, and particularly in the 1960s and 1970s, the migration of people from outside Europe increased enormously. The West became the destination for large numbers of immigrants from developing regions, such as India and Africa.

In 1947, two years after the end of the Second World War, people queue outside an airline office in London, waiting to start their journey to a new life in Canada.

PERSPECTIVES

Xiaojun (Debbie), aged 13, describes moving from China to America in the early 1990s:

'My new teacher asked "Does she have an English name? No? Well, what about Debbie?" That's how I got my name… Coming to America has changed my life. Now my parents work too hard and I never see them. But we do have a TV, a radio, a microwave, and a washing machine.'

(*Source:* Closing the Borders *by Wendy Davies, 1995*)

PERSPECTIVES

'The world's dominant economy, and one of the richest, is the United States – a country populated almost entirely by immigrants and their descendants. The US population has doubled over the last century, yet the country has become wealthier and wealthier.'

Peter Stalker, consultant to a number of UN agencies and author of two books on migration for the International Labour Organization, quoted in The No-Nonsense Guide to International Migration, *2000*

Wooing the workers

After the war, many countries that had been European colonies gained their freedom. But most of their people remained desperately poor. The European economies were expanding fast, and urgently needed workers. They relied on immigrants from their former colonies to work in their factories, health services and transport systems.

Each country tended to recruit labour from its former colonies. For instance, the UK sought workers from the Caribbean and South Asia. Germany had no former colonies but invited in Turkish, Italian, Greek, Portuguese and North African people.

The Gulf States, especially Saudi Arabia, Kuwait and the United Arab Emirates, were developing their economies too. South and East Asians, and a large number of Africans, answered the call for labour. Workers from neighbouring Arab countries came too.

From the 1960s onwards, the USA, Australia and Canada relaxed their immigration rules. They admitted many more people from developing countries, rather than just Europeans as previously.

Between 1965 and 1996, 20.1 million migrants, mostly from Latin American and Asian countries, came to the USA. It was only when their economies were no longer doing so well that the developed countries began to question whether immigration was a good thing.

Forced to flee – refugees

Throughout history, there have always been refugees. Since Roman times, Jewish people have regularly been expelled from countries and forced to move on. In sixteenth- and seventeenth-century Europe, thousands of French Protestants, called

---

Estimated percentage of migrants from developing countries admitted to Australia, Canada and the USA in the early 1960s and the late 1980s

Australia
- Early 1960s: 7.8 per cent
- Late 1980s: 53.7 per cent

Canada
- Early 1960s: 12.3 per cent
- Late 1980s: 70.8 per cent

USA
- Early 1960s: 41.1 per cent
- Late 1980s: 87.9 per cent

(Source: W. M. Spellman, Professor of History, University of North Carolina, USA, author of The Global Community: migration and the making of the modern world, *2002)*

Huguenots, fled to Britain, the Netherlands and Switzerland. They had been persecuted for their religious beliefs in Catholic France. Refugees sometimes suffered on arrival too (Jewish people were often treated badly), yet the Huguenots were welcomed. And in 1832, a French law stated that money should be given to important refugees!

During the late nineteenth century, Jewish people suffered terrible anti-Semitism in Russia and eastern Europe. Blamed for their countries' problems, they were subjected to organized violent attacks. Between 1880 and 1929, over 3.5 million Jews fled – mostly to the USA, and also Europe. (Only a small minority moved to Palestine.) At first they met with suspicion and distrust but nevertheless succeeded in making a new life for themselves.

The first half of the twentieth century was a grim period of world wars and economic depression. Both the First and Second World

Refugee children, mostly Jewish, arriving in the UK from Vienna, Austria, in 1938. Their parents sent them to safety in Britain because they feared for their lives in Nazi-occupied Austria.

PERSPECTIVES

Margot, a Jewish woman, escaped from Germany as a child in 1939:

'I lived through the terror of *Kristallnacht* [the violence against Jews and their property that occurred throughout Germany and Austria on 9-10 November 1938] and saw my father taken away to Dachau [concentration camp] and so it seems strange to me now that I was very excited by the prospect of going to England to live with strangers. I was taken in by a young family... I was housed and fed but never loved... The ending of my story is a happy one. My parents survived and arrived in the United States in September 1941. I had preceded them in May 1940.'

(Source: I Came Alone *compiled by Bertha Leverton and Shmuel Lowensohn, 1990)*

Wars forced millions to leave their homes. During the Second World War, over 60 million people from Nazi-occupied Europe became refugees within Europe – and some of them never managed to return home.

Bitter conflicts

Following the Second World War, many countries in Asia and Africa that had been colonies fought for their independence. The conflicts led to huge movements of people. When the British finally left India in 1947, the country was divided. India became a secular (non-religious) nation with a majority of Hindus, while Pakistan became a Muslim country. Following partition, at least 10 million Hindus, Muslims and Sikhs switched countries, hoping to reach safety. During that tragic migration, one million people were slaughtered by those of a different religion.

Palestinian refugee children at one of the large refugee camps in Jericho, West Bank, in 1949. They had had to leave their homes when the State of Israel was formed in 1948.

Further upheavals included the flight of 750,000 Palestinian refugees when Israel was established, and the subsequent movement of Jewish people from Arab countries to Israel. When Communism spread to eastern Europe and China after the Second World War, millions fled, because they were not prepared to live under this system.

The Cold War and after

The post-war pattern of mass flight was set to continue. Since the 1950s, over 95 per cent of refugee movements have come from the developing world – usually the poorest countries.

During the 1960s and 1970s, wars of independence against European rule were fought in African countries, for example in Algeria (1954-62). Algerians fled to neighbouring Morocco and Tunisia.

The 1970s brought crises in Asia, with large-scale conflicts in Cambodia, Laos and Vietnam creating massive waves of refugees. These were related to the Cold War. The USSR and the USA

Thousands of Rwandan refugees returning to Rwanda from Tanzania in 1996. They had fled to Tanzania in 1994 following the genocide.

CASE STUDY

Eight-year-old Ghada and her family lived in Qatamon in West Jerusalem, Palestine. By April 1948, it had become too dangerous to stay there. With bombings and shootings on a daily basis, most Palestinians had already left. Finally, Ghada and her family could take no more. Fortunate to find a taxi driver, they quickly jumped into the car and sped off, with explosions going off around them. They drove to Damascus in Syria and in 1949 flew to Britain, where Ghada's father had managed to get a job.

Ghada grew up Arab inside the home and English outside. As a child, she wanted to be as English as possible. Yet she felt she somehow did not belong. When she grew up she visited Arab countries but now she did not belong there either. Like millions of refugees, she lived a divided life.

(Based on Ghada Karmi: In Search of Fatima*)*

PERSPECTIVES

'The war in Somalia was awful, they were killing people and raping women. We had to leave, we had no choice. I think people believe we want to come here to get a free house and a mobile phone. But these are lies.'

Somali refugee, UK, 2003

fought for influence over different countries by allying themselves with opposing warring groups. The USA lost the struggle to control Vietnam and a Communist government took power across the land. Many Vietnamese refugees fled to the USA and Australia to avoid living under Communism. When Fidel Castro came to power in Cuba in 1959, many escaped to the USA for the same reason; more followed in the Mariel boatlift of the late 1970s and in other escapes from Castro's Cuba.

An American plane returns to the USA from Cuba in 1961, bringing 86 refugees from Communist Cuba. Most of the refugees were afraid to speak openly about their experiences in case Castro's regime took revenge on their relatives in Cuba.

The 1980s and 1990s were no better. Armed conflict in Rwanda, Somalia, Afghanistan and the Balkans led to the forced migration of millions. The figures are unimaginably large. Six million Afghan refugees fled after the USSR sent troops to invade Afghanistan in 1979. And in 1994, two million Rwandans escaped from their country following the horrifying genocide in which more than a million people were murdered.

All over the world, millions of people have been caught up in complex crises, which can sometimes go on for decades. Many have to flee for their lives more than once.

DEBATE

Should refugees fleeing persecution individually, because of their religion, ethnic group or beliefs, be seen in a different light from people fleeing as a group from a war raging in their country?

3: The Economics of Migration

Imagine someone working on the land and finding out that he can earn twice as much money if he moves to the city. Would he be tempted? Almost certainly. Most migration is actually within countries, for this kind of reason. In the same way, it is quite natural for people from poorer countries to migrate to a neighbouring country – or even further afield. This happens between poor Poland and rich Germany, between Malaysia and Singapore, and between Mexico and the USA. A Polish factory worker can go to Germany and earn three times his or her monthly wage, and the average factory worker in the USA earns around four times as much as he or she would in Mexico.

Migration experts talk about 'push and pull factors'. The push factors are the bad things in a person's country that make him or

This girl and her poverty-stricken family live in a disused railway carriage, Mexico.

PERSPECTIVES

Ana Amaral, from Angola, lost her job in Brazil, when a US company bought the firm. She went to work as a cleaner in the USA:

'It's globalization. The Americans came to my country and so now I am here ... I can't go back because people are dependent on me for money.'

(Source: Guardian *newspaper, UK, 3 October 2003)*

her want to leave. The 'pull' factors are the good things about another country that encourage a person to migrate there.

Economics plays a major part in the decision to migrate. Over the last two decades there has been a process of globalization. Faster and cheaper transport and communications have allowed powerful transnational companies to produce goods and run services wherever they like in the world, generally at the lowest cost. They argue that this creates wealth that will trickle down through society, improving everyone's lives, down to the very poorest.

However, some believe that this process has actually increased the gap between rich and poor. Nowadays, 85 per cent of the global population live in a country where the rich–poor divide is growing. They see the way of life in wealthy countries, which has become increasingly visible to them through the media. It is no surprise that people in poor countries are 'pushed' to move if they can. Yet the vast majority cannot afford to migrate.

Shaking up lives

Economic changes can certainly push people to migrate. For instance, in Mexico the government used to provide subsidies to cut costs for farmers. When these subsidies were reduced in the 1980s, Mexican farmers had to charge more for their produce. The market was then flooded with cheap, subsidized food from the USA. Many Mexican farmers were put out of business and ended up working as labourers on farms in the USA or migrating to cities in Mexico or the US.

This legal immigrant from Brazil works as a housekeeper in Arlington, Virginia, USA. She earns far more than she would in Brazil.

Nevertheless, money does not decide everything. There are other 'pull' factors, such as wanting a better, freer life in a more democratic country. Immigrants are usually the most adventurous people, often young men, and sometimes young women, who have the loosest family ties. They are willing to take their chances in a new place. Nowadays, faster and cheaper transport makes it easier to get to other countries – if you can afford the fare. Mobile phones enable you to stay in touch with people back home once you are there. Everyone has his or her own personal reasons for wanting to go elsewhere. But generally, the evidence shows that people will move if they know there will be plenty of work for them once they arrive.

Is immigration good for the host country?

Immigrants generally travel well-worn paths, following members of their own community who have gone before. They often have a job already lined up, and stay with friends or relatives until they can set up home. A major destination is the USA, which has immigrants from around the globe – around 12.5 per cent of the population are of Hispanic origin and 3.6 per cent Asian. Refugees are also keen to work and usually have skills to offer.

An immigrant worker cleaning the street in Saudi Arabia.

PERSPECTIVES

'It is not the poor who move, not those from either the poorest countries or the poorest areas in the countries where immigrants come from. The overwhelming majority stay at home... Blaming poverty is a cop-out to hide the real reason for migration. Europe and North America need the workers.'

Nigel Harris, Professor of Urban Economics, University College, London

CASE STUDY

Héctor Liñán left Mexico for the USA all alone, aged 18, without knowing any English. He headed for Chicago, where his first job was washing dishes in a restaurant.

Three years later, Héctor returned to Mexico, and got married. He and his wife Andrea went to the USA together. He says, 'I was [there] illegally, but after three years, all the restaurant owners were after me to work for them. I was a good cook and I spoke English and Greek too.' He later set up his own snack bar with two employees.

(Source: Mexican Migration Project)

The newcomers tend to do the jobs that local people are not prepared to do. These jobs are known as the '3 Ds' because they are 'dirty, dangerous and difficult'. In the Gulf States, for instance, huge numbers of foreign domestic servants clean up after their employers. In the UK, about 70 per cent of people working in London's catering industry, providing food for the city, are immigrants. And around 80 per cent of the coffee in the Dominican Republic is picked by Haitians.

In addition, there are the skilled immigrants, desperately needed in Europe and North America. In 2000, for example, Germany introduced a scheme to bring in IT professionals from outside Europe. The population of the developed countries is ageing; in 2050, Europe will have an average age of 53. Immigrants tend to be young and well educated, helping to increase the workforce.

The statistics generally show that immigrants are good for the host economy. They tend to contribute more in taxes than they use in welfare services. Some surveys show that, at worst, immigrants make little difference to the economy.

An immigrant healthcare worker looks after an elderly woman in the USA. Many of the low-paid staff working at homes for the elderly are immigrants.

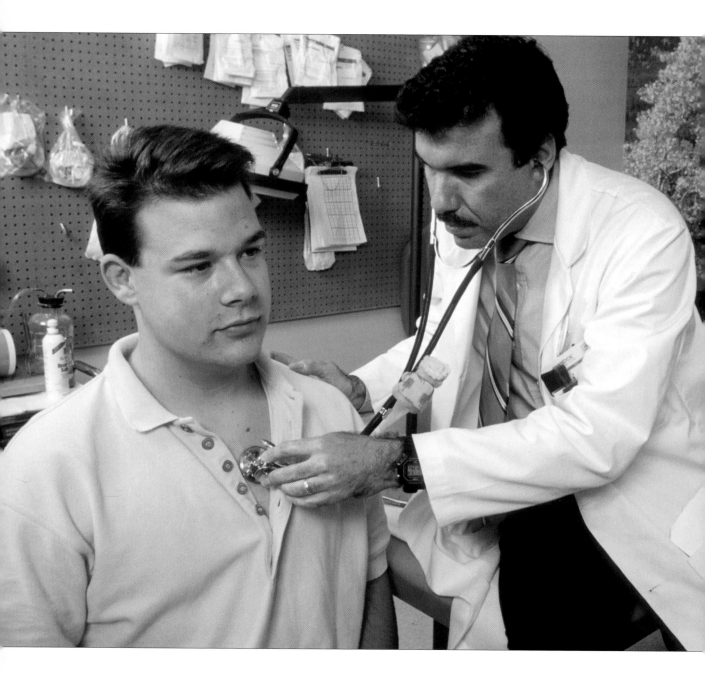

Is migration good for the sending country?

For many families, having a family member working abroad is a lifeline. They simply could not manage without the remittances – the sums of money that migrant workers send back home to their families. Some countries' economies depend on this money. In the Philippines, about 15 per cent of households receive income from abroad. In Lesotho, southern Africa, a full quarter of Gross Domestic Product comes from migrants! Sometimes, however, migrants find they cannot send back money as planned because their living costs are very high.

An immigrant doctor treats a patient in Virginia, USA.

PERSPECTIVES

'Migration of medical professionals from developing countries has become a major concern... In Africa alone, where health needs ... are greatest, around 23,000 qualified academic professionals emigrate annually... The loss of nurses has been even more extreme; for example, more than 150,000 Filipino nurses and 18,000 Zimbabwean nurses work abroad.'

(*Source:* British Medical Journal, *2002*)

When many educated people, such as teachers or doctors, leave to work abroad, it can cause problems in their home country – this is sometimes called the 'brain drain'. Jamaica is a good example; three-quarters of people who have been to university have left the country. Migration can have a damaging effect on the families they leave. Generally, women are left to care for families alone when their partners migrate.

Do refugees help the host country's economy?

In developed countries, refugees form a tiny percentage of the population. The cost to the country of caring for them is relatively small. Refugees in developed countries are often highly skilled people and can make a significant contribution to the economy. Yet they may not be allowed to work in the host country because their qualifications are not recognized. In 2003, this was the case for 3,000 refugee doctors in the UK.

In developing countries, refugees may have a mixed effect on the economic situation. The arrival of large numbers of refugees in one place can severely strain resources. However, their demand for services can also boost the economy. For example, until the 1990s, the Tanzanian town of Kibondo was a poor village. After the arrival of Rwandan refugees in 1994 it developed into a busy town, with better schools and clinics for local people as well as refugees. The refugees created a bigger market for goods too. When they left, local merchants grumbled, 'Now we have no one to sell our bananas to.'

DEBATE

Even if immigration is good for the economy, should governments still have immigration controls so they can control who comes into their country?

4: A Political Hot Potato

Between the 1940s and 1970s, governments in developed countries encouraged people from abroad to come to work (see pages 12-13). Then, economic problems started and people began to lose their jobs. Far-right political parties blamed immigrants – they believed their country should just be for 'their own people'. During the 1995 presidential elections in France, for example, far-right leader Jean-Marie Le Pen declared that deporting (sending back) three million immigrants would solve the problem of three million jobless French people. In fact the economy is more complicated than that, but simple solutions can seem attractive. Since the 1970s, many governments in developed countries have tightened their laws limiting immigration.

Making the move: legal immigrants

Nowadays it is very hard to move to a developed country legally unless you are skilled. Several countries, such as the UK, Germany, Canada and Australia, offer special visas for highly qualified people such as doctors. The USA allows the entry of a quota of immigrants each year, as does Russia. Immigrants who

Members of the far-right National Front marching through central London, UK, in 1980.

CASE STUDY

Albert, a 40-year old Filipino, entered Israel with a visa that meant he could work for his employer for two years. He was also provided with a residence permit, allowing him to live in Israel for the period of the visa. However, he was not allowed to change jobs. Albert's employer was old and sick and unfortunately died. Albert lost his work visa and ended up in prison as an illegal immigrant.

(*Source:* Double Crossings: Migration Now, *published by Index on Censorship, 2003*)

are already living in a developed country can become citizens after living there for five years or more, depending on the individual country.

Israel and immigration

Unlike most other developed nations, Israel positively seeks immigrants. In the 1990s, after the collapse of the Soviet Union, up to one million immigrants arrived! Today, one in six Israelis come from the former USSR. There is still a labour shortage, yet the Israeli government does not wish to employ the local Palestinians to fill the gap because of the conflict between the two peoples. Instead it welcomes temporary workers from Thailand, the Philippines, China, eastern Europe and South America. They receive a visa linked to a particular job. And if they change jobs, they lose the right to stay.

Developing countries

It is still easier to migrate legally to developing countries, where controls are generally less strict. Governments in countries that send migrants, especially in Asia, often help to organize workers to go. For instance, many Chinese migrant workers are to be found working in developing countries such as South Korea.

What happens to undocumented immigrants?

For those who cannot get to their desired country legally, there are difficult and dangerous illegal ways. Imagine being so desperate to get to a European country that you risk your life to sail there in a tiny boat over stormy seas, with little food or water and just the clothes you are standing in. You have spent all your meagre savings to pay a 'people smuggler' to arrange the trip. Your family is relying on you making it alive. You know that if you get caught you will simply be sent back.

Some people take unbelievable risks. They may cling on underneath a train or even a plane to try to reach their destination. They could be sealed in a container in the hold of a ship or locked in the back of a lorry. They will be lucky to survive the journey.

In many countries, immigrants who are caught without a visa are sent straight back to their country of origin. This is what happens to Moroccans found by the Spanish authorities trying to cross the Strait of Gibraltar, for example. In Australia, undocumented immigrants and asylum seekers are put into detention while their cases are decided. However, undocumented immigrants may also be refugees who do not know how to claim asylum.

Undocumented immigrants on a Spanish patrol boat after being rescued from a boat near the coast of southern Spain. They will be returned to the countries they came from.

PERSPECTIVES

'I've tried the *pateras* [little fishing boats] three times. Once we were arrested, twice we capsized. Six people died but I'd try it again. If I die I'll be an economic martyr. Everything I do is for my family.'

A survivor of the sea crossing from Morocco to Spain, interviewed by the Association of Friends and Families of Victims of Clandestine Immigration

'One of the reasons the Department of Security was created is to prevent the wrong applicant from receiving an immigration benefit. Our comprehensive background checks, and effective risk management, sorts out the bad apples. Our initiatives for dramatically refreshing the citizenship process … will cultivate the good ones.'

Eduardo Aguirre, Director of US Citizenship and Immigration Services, November 2003

Immigrants may succeed in arriving illegally. For example, they may arrive in the USA from Latin American countries and be absorbed into the local Hispanic community. Eventually, after spending several years in the country, they may be accepted and allowed to remain legally. Illegal (undocumented) immigrants present a tricky issue for governments. On the one hand governments clamp down on them, but on the other hand the immigrants are useful to the economy. They do the jobs no one else wants to do – and for less money.

Developing countries have also tried to restrict immigration. For example, in 1999, Bangladesh launched a drive to seek out at least 100,000 illegal foreign workers. India deports illegal immigrants, although not if they can prove they will be tortured if sent back. Malaysia has a particularly harsh policy. Illegal immigrant workers are punished with six strokes of a cane before being thrown into prison. But because border controls are generally less strict, it is still easier to get into developing countries.

An Iraqi refugee and his three-year-old daughter wait at a refugee camp in France, hoping to reach England.

What are government policies towards refugees?

If people have to escape their country, where are they likely to go? The chances are, that they will go to the nearest country they can get to – or maybe to a place where they

PERSPECTIVES

'We are not advocating a "Fortress Europe". But there has to be some order and some rules brought into the system whereby people come into Europe.'

British Prime Minister, Tony Blair, 2002

have family. For these reasons, most refugees come from poor countries and go to other poor countries. Africa and Asia receive four-fifths of the world's refugees.

Poorer countries, which have historically welcomed refugees, have now toughened their stance. Iran is one of them. With a population of 68 million in 2003, Iran has around two million refugees. When US-led forces attacked Afghanistan in 2001 (because Afghanistan's leaders were believed to be sheltering terrorists), Iran and other neighbouring countries quickly closed their borders to new arrivals as they already had so many

Afghan refugees on a bus at a border post between Iran and Afghanistan, on their way back to their home country.

refugees. The Iranian government encourages Afghans to leave. They are not allowed to participate fully in Iranian society; for example, in 2003, Afghan children were not allowed to enrol in school. However, Iran's harsh stance should be seen in the light of the fact that it has such a high proportion of refugees.

Applying for asylum

The issue of refugees is hotly debated in developed countries too, although far fewer refugees make their way to them. Governments have an asylum system to control who can stay in the country. This is based on the 1951 Convention (see page 6) but it is hard to apply. It can be difficult to judge if someone is an economic migrant or a refugee. The 1951 Convention on refugees does not include people fleeing poverty, however life-threatening it may be. Nor does it consider people to be refugees if they are persecuted because of their gender or their sexuality.

Many refugees have to flee quickly, without passports or visas. Often they do not know the rules for applying for asylum. They are seen as illegal immigrants or 'bogus' asylum seekers if they cannot prove that they are refugees. Austria, Ireland, Italy, the USA, the UK and the Netherlands are just some of the countries that have tightened up the rules to actively discourage asylum seekers. For instance, the UK lists countries believed to be 'safe'. If you come from one of them, you are very unlikely to get asylum. This can be problematic. For example, in 2003, Afghanistan was listed as a safe country even though it was still in chaos after the 2001 war.

The political situation has an impact too. Following the terrorist attacks of 11 September 2001, Americans experienced heightened fears that asylum seekers could be terrorists. In fiscal (tax) years 2002 and 2003, the USA drastically reduced its intake of refugees, from a target of 70,000 to only 27,508 and 28,419 respectively.

PERSPECTIVES

'We came back because we heard there was peace and security. But there is no work and no place we can afford to live. We have freedom now, but we cannot eat that.'

One of nearly two million Afghan refugees who have returned to Afghanistan, 2002

CASE STUDY

A young refugee from the Democratic Republic of Congo says:

'I'm the eldest of five brothers and sisters... We had an uncle in Europe who was a refugee and against Mobutu [the president]. He sent us clothes and cassettes about anti-Mobutu demonstrations in Europe. The neighbours saw the cassettes and thought we were anti-Mobutu. For three years our house was targeted by soldiers who took whatever they could. We often had to hide in the countryside to escape them.

'...our uncle in Europe had us brought to Kinshasa [the capital] where we felt scared... It was a long time before our uncle could get us out... It is our country ... but after all the dangers we faced it was good to get out. We were aged 11 to 17 when we left.'

(*Source:* Separated Children Coming to Western Europe, *Save the Children Fund, 2000*)

This was mainly because of increased security measures, which delayed the process of applying for resettlement and meant that many refugees who had been cleared to come to the USA were not permitted to enter the country. In 2003, Iraqi refugees were being kept out; for example, 300 Iraqi refugees in Lebanon who had been approved by US interviewers were not allowed to travel to the USA.

What happens to asylum seekers?

In developing countries, groups of refugees fleeing conflict or persecution are usually accepted as a group. After the massacre of over a million people in 1994, about 400,000 Rwandan refugees fled to Tanzania, Burundi and Zaire (now the Democratic Republic of the Congo). No one asked each one to explain his or her reason for fleeing.

In developed countries, such as in the USA, Europe or Australia, individuals generally need to make their own claim for asylum. In the USA, applicants are not allowed to work but receive no welfare benefits while they are waiting to find out if their asylum

Two protesters demonstrate outside the Woomera Refugee Centre, in Australia, where undocumented immigrants and asylum seekers are detained.

claim will be granted. Those deemed to have entered the country illegally are detained. Others have to rely on their own funds, or friends, family or charity, to support them. In the UK, it is essential for asylum seekers to make a claim on arrival, otherwise they will not receive any help with housing or living costs. The authorities then assess whether they believe they really have been persecuted. If the authorities decide that they are telling the truth, they may be permitted to stay in the country. However, sometimes it is hard for asylum seekers to prove what has happened to them, and they may be turned down.

In Australia, all asylum seekers, including children, are placed in detention centres while their claims are processed. The government argues that otherwise they may disappear and could not be forced to leave if their claims were turned down.

European countries also place some asylum seekers in detention centres. Others may be housed together in one area, or spread out around the country. Asylum seekers usually want to work, but generally it is easier to get welfare benefits than permission to work.

Some children are forced to seek refuge in a foreign land on their own. Perhaps their parents have died, or have sent them away – believing it to be their only chance of survival. Afraid, alone, often not speaking the language, they will be taken into the care of the local authorities on arrival.

This 18-year-old Iraqi is seeking asylum in Denmark. His father has been sent back to Iraq.

DEBATE

According to the 1951 UN Convention, a refugee is a person who has left his or her own country 'owing to a well-founded fear of being persecuted for reasons of race, nationality, membership of a particular social group or political opinion.' How do you think the Convention should be applied – tightly or generously?

5: Immigrants and Refugees in Society

Most refugees flee in a desperate hurry, terrified for their lives, leaving everything behind. Over half the world's refugees are children. They may have had horrific experiences – perhaps members of their family were murdered in front of their eyes.

Life in a new country – for refugees

As a refugee, you may be one of the minority that travel across continents. You arrive in a strange country, you do not speak the language and you have no idea what to do next. You could even be a child alone.

Being a refugee affects your education. Many refugees have to flee more than once and spend many years away from home. In Africa and Asia, the average amount of time a child is displaced from home is six years. During that time, he or she might not receive any education. Yet moving away may sometimes have a positive effect. For example, Afghan refugee girls who fled to Pakistan in the 1990s were able to go to school there. (In Afghanistan under Taliban rule, from the mid-1990s to 2001, girls were not allowed to go to school.)

Life in a new country – for immigrants

You face challenges if you are an immigrant. If you decide to move voluntarily, you may have friends or family to welcome you and provide a roof over your head. But some people have no one to go to. Generally, immigrants end up living in the poorest

CASE STUDY

Mr Aldana paid $1,000 to a trafficker to take his son Lorenzo from Guatemala to the USA, but the trafficker left him stranded in Mexico. Lorenzo worked there for a year to save the money to complete the journey; 17 years later he remains in the USA as an illegal immigrant. He says:

'I didn't want to go back to Guatemala. I am the oldest son and I had to get to America to support my family.'

(Source: Guardian newspaper, UK, 3 October 2003)

housing. The food and climate may be different and it might be hard to find food, music and other familiar things you had in your country. You will miss your home and want to keep up with what is going on there. You will probably need to learn a new language too. Children learn quite quickly at school but it still takes time to fit in and be accepted.

Being an immigrant can be a positive experience. Canada, for example, prides itself on being a genuinely multicultural country, a mosaic of peoples from around the world. But it is still hard for newcomers at first. Highly qualified people realize they cannot get jobs practising their professions. A doctor may have to work as a taxi driver, an accountant as a cleaner. Yet those who stay on generally have a better life in the end – especially the younger generation. Healthcare is free and the standard of education is high, as is the quality of homes and transport.

Success in a new land

Where do your favourite TV, film and music stars, and sports personalities come from? Many famous Hollywood film actors are immigrants. For instance, Arnold Schwarzenegger started life in Austria and Salma Hayek was born in Mexico. In 2003, top footballer David Beckham left the UK to play for Real Madrid

Afghan girls at school in Pakistan in 1995. After the end of Taliban rule in 2001, girls were once more allowed to go to school in Aghanistan. By autumn 2003, one million girls were receiving education, out of a total of 4.2 million school children.

THE LEARNING CENTRE
TOWER HAMLETS COLLEGE
POPLAR CENTRE
POPLAR HIGH STREET
LONDON E14 0AF

in Spain. So he is an economic migrant! Some refugees and immigrants achieve huge success. Sabeer Bhatia left India for the USA in 1988 with $200 to his name. He invented Hotmail, which he sold to Microsoft for $10 million ten years later. Famous refugees include the artist Marc Chagall (1887-1985), a Jewish refugee from Belarus, eastern Europe, and Madeleine Albright, from Czechoslovakia, who became US Secretary of State in 1997.

The lure of migration

On the other hand, things can go disastrously wrong. Poor people in developing countries may know of opportunities to work in wealthier countries but may not know how to get there. They can fall victim to people traffickers. For example, traffickers tell young girls in South-East Asia that they will take them to a well-paid job abroad. They lure them to Thailand and force them into sex work. Alone in a strange country, often threatened with violence by the traffickers, they have little choice but to oblige. Their families are counting on them to send back money.

Others, such as Filipino women in the Gulf States or Hong Kong, take jobs as domestic workers but are treated more like slaves. Migration may offer the promise of good money but the reality may be quite different.

Madeleine Albright, former US Secretary of State, was born in Czechoslovakia and arrived in the USA at the age of 11. She came from a Jewish family and they were twice forced to flee, once by the Nazis and once by the Communists.

PERSPECTIVES

'Marinella', a Romanian woman, went to Italy expecting to find a job in a pizzeria:

'The girls all wanted to get to Italy to work as photo models, as cooks or in hotels. They had been promised large sums of money. When I heard ... that we were going to be sold and become prostitutes, I couldn't believe my ears. I tried to kill myself. For one and a half months I couldn't call home. I have a little girl... I didn't think I'd ever get home.'

(*Source:* Double Crossings, *Index on Censorship*, 2003)

A fear of foreigners

How would you feel if someone from another country joined your class at school? Nowadays, as countries around the world restrict the numbers of immigrants and refugees, why are people so anxious about newcomers?

There is a fear in developed countries that too many people are coming and there will not be room for them all. For example,

CASE STUDY

A young Filipino woman, Cathy is the youngest of six children. Her mother is a widow. Cathy hoped to study management and start a business but her mother could not afford the college fees. Cathy decided to earn the money in Hong Kong.

She found an employer through her sister, who had already worked in Hong Kong. Ms Leung told Cathy she would be treated like a 'younger sister'. But she was forced to work 16 hours a day: washing, shopping, cooking, cleaning, and caring for two dogs. She had to clean other people's flats too. She did not even receive a proper wage. Cathy was often given leftovers to eat and slept in a sweltering hot storeroom. For an immigrant domestic worker, Cathy's situation was not unusual.

(*Source: Nicole Constable,* Guardian *newspaper, UK, 14 July 2003*)

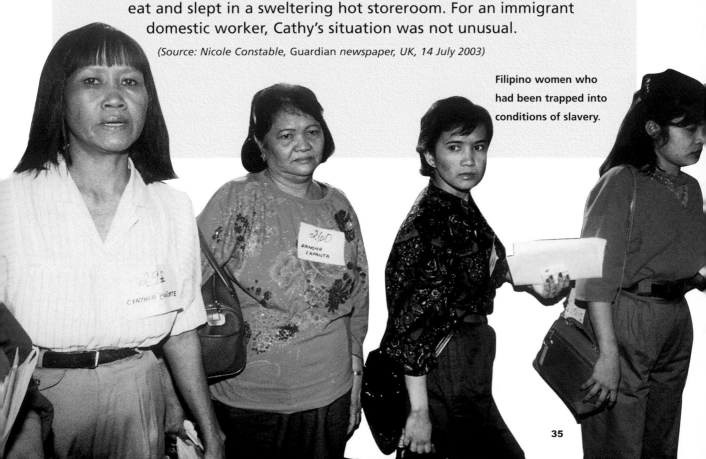

Filipino women who had been trapped into conditions of slavery.

those living in run-down housing estates, in areas where health, education and social services are stretched, may worry that immigrants and refugees will take away resources and jobs from local residents. These fears are by no means restricted to poorer people; better-off people express them too.

A newer fear is that refugees and immigrants could be criminals or even terrorists. If they have no legal documents, how do you

In this run-down suburb in Paris, France, resentment and tension can easily develop.

PERSPECTIVES

In September 2001, Peter Reith, Australian Minister for Defence, said:

'[There's a need to] manage people coming into your country. You've got to be able to control that; otherwise it can be a pipeline for terrorists to come in and use your country as a staging post for terrorist activities.'

know who you are letting in? This fear has increased hugely since the terrorist attacks of 11 September 2001 in the USA.

Another problem is that of identifying refugees. How do you know that they are genuine? Perhaps they are economic migrants, pretending they have suffered persecution in order to take advantage of the asylum system? Yet another argument concerns cultural differences. The newcomers have other customs, speak foreign languages, practise different religions. Does that mean that they will 'swamp' the local culture and traditions?

Calming the fears

As this book shows, many of these fears are not grounded in reality. It is generally in countries where the fewest people arrive that concern is greatest. Immigrants usually benefit the economy. There is often an increase in crime when immigrants arrive – but it tends to take the form of racist attacks against the newcomers rather than crime committed by them. Also, people focus on the arrival of immigrants and refugees, but they never talk about the millions who leave. In 2002, for example, over two million refugees returned to Afghanistan.

Newcomers usually adapt to the host culture, which becomes richer and more varied as a result. In the major cities of the USA,

Members of an Afghan family sit on the steps of JFK International Airport, having just arrived in the USA. They may be treated with suspicion because of their appearance, customs and religious beliefs.

you can find food from all around the globe. Think of the variety in the music scene that has developed with the influence of traditions from Africa, Asia and the Middle East. Arts, theatre, dance – all areas of culture have drawn inspiration from a changing population.

From ignorance to abuse

People's fears of immigrants and refugees have a real effect. In developed countries, many have lost faith in the mainstream political parties to improve their lives. Far-right parties are taking up some of the issues that people worry about. For example, they claim to be concerned about bad housing, lack of doctors, and shortage of teachers. But, rather than looking at the complex causes of these problems, they simply blame immigrants and refugees for taking up resources.

In response, many mainstream political parties have simply accepted these arguments and restricted the numbers of

London's annual Notting Hill Carnival was originally an Afro-Caribbean event but nowadays the celebrations are enjoyed by people from many different backgrounds.

PERSPECTIVES

'Politicians have a choice to make. They can embrace the potential that immigrants and refugees represent or they can use them as political scapegoats.'

Kofi Annan, UN Secretary-General, 2003

immigrants and refugees. In the Netherlands in 2002, far-right politician Pim Fortuyn, leader of the List Pim Fortuyn Party, opposed immigration. He argued that the country was 'full up', even though the birth rate was falling. Fortuyn was murdered in May 2002, but his party's views had a significant impact on Dutch politics. Due to changes in asylum policy, in 2002 the Netherlands fell from the sixth to the eleventh largest net receiver of refugees in Europe.

With political parties disapproving of immigrants and refugees, it is no surprise that there is an increase in racism on the street. This can range from nasty name-calling to violent attacks. In Australia in 2003, for example, a Muslim woman who chooses to wear the veil reported: 'I was shopping at Kogarah in the centre and someone threw eggs at me, spat at me and took my veil off.' A rise in anti-Muslim sentiment in the USA after the 11 September attacks led to brutal racist murders of Muslims – and hundreds of assaults on Sikhs because their attackers thought they were Muslims.

Trouble starts to flare up in a school playground in Texas, USA. Racism can often be a factor in teenage bullying.

Building bridges between communities

Many people are horrified by such ignorance and violence, and work to build good community relations. After the murder in 2001 of Kurdish asylum seeker Firsat Yildiz in Sighthill, Scotland, money was put into improving housing and the youth centre, and multicultural festivals were organized. Relations

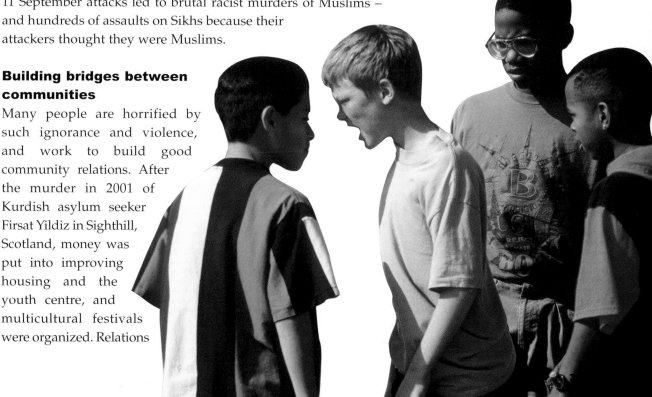

between asylum seekers and local people improved, although there was still much work to be done.

Refugees have good experiences too. Kemal Pervanic is a Bosnian Muslim. He was pictured on the news, a painfully thin prisoner in a Serb concentration camp during the Bosnian war in 1992. He fled to the UK as a refugee in 1993 and completed a science degree, securing a future for himself. There are still success stories, but things are generally becoming harder for refugees in Europe.

Myth and reality in the media

What have you seen on TV, magazines and newspapers about immigrants and refugees? Does the reporting give you different sides of the debate? The media often sensationalize the issues by focusing on newcomers as a threat, which can cause anxiety among the host population.

Such negative media coverage is nothing new. In the 1900s, racist attitudes towards Jewish immigrants were to be found in the press, for example in Britain. Seen as dirty and greedy, there were complaints that too many were arriving. Between 1933 and 1945, millions of European Jews attempted to escape the terror of Nazi rule. Nowadays, it is widely accepted that they were genuine refugees. Yet at the time, they were treated with hostility as well as sympathy.

Today, much of the media contribute to fear and hatred of asylum seekers. In Ireland, for example, it is common to refer to asylum seekers as a 'flood' or 'tide', which is 'swamping' the country. In 2002, Irish TV showed footage of long queues of asylum seekers outside the Refugee Applications Centre in the

PERSPECTIVES

'Biased media coverage has been alleged by many consultation participants: "[They] don't focus on crimes of non-Arabs but focus only on crimes committed by Arabs." There is a lot of dissatisfaction with current anti-discrimination legislation, which allows most journalists and broadcasters to get away with direct racist statements.'

Isma, National Consultations on Eliminating Prejudice against Arab and Muslim Australians, 2003

capital, Dublin. The images were actually filmed in 1999, at a time when staff shortages were causing delays!

Reports in the media can affect people's ideas. For instance, a UK survey in 2000 showed that people believed asylum seekers received £113 ($63) a week – the real figure was £36.54 ($20). Inaccurate reporting can fuel resentment, which in turn can lead to verbal or even physical attacks on refugees.

Positive viewpoints

Parts of the media do play a positive role. Some newspapers, TV programmes and voluntary organizations produce carefully researched materials which communicate the facts about refugees and migrants. For example, to counteract increased racism against Arabs and Muslims in Australia, the anti-racist organization, Isma, is working with the Press Council to encourage fair, accurate and balanced reporting about Muslim and Arab Australians.

Immigrants themselves use their talents to produce their own media. In California, USA, one-third of the population is Hispanic, about 12 per cent is Asian, and there are dozens of other groups. New California Media is a news service that brings news and views from their homelands to English speakers. Translators monitor media from places including the Middle East, India, China and Mexico. Mainstream journalists then pick up on the stories. In this way, the various immigrants' contributions and experiences enrich the media as a whole.

The editor of the Vietnamese daily newspaper, *Chieu Duong*, which is produced in Sydney, Australia. In Sydney, there are also several Chinese newspapers, as well as a Jewish and a Catholic newspaper.

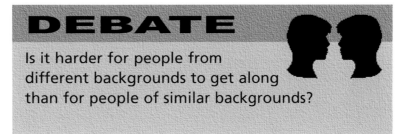

DEBATE

Is it harder for people from different backgrounds to get along than for people of similar backgrounds?

6: Where Do We Go from Here?

While the world is divided into rich and poor countries (and within them rich and poor regions), people will continue to migrate for a better life. The process of globalization is changing economies and people's lives all over the world. Transnational companies like McDonalds and the Ford Motor Company set up businesses and factories in any country they choose. So, should people have the right to go anywhere? (If you have plenty of money, you can! According to the rules of the Canadian Immigrant Investor program, set up in 1986, immigrants who have the required financial resources may settle freely in Canada. In 2003, they had to possess $500,000 and be able to invest $250,000.)

If all immigration were legal, it would certainly be easier to identify immigrants' needs and help them to settle. For example, they could be helped to learn the language of their host country.

This asylum seeker in Denmark knows only 100 Danish words, compared to the 10,000 words an average Danish child of his age would know. He shows great enthusiasm for learning and will probably speak Danish very soon.

PERSPECTIVES

'Going back to Somalia would be to plunge back into the flames. Going to America is a dream. It is the choice between the fire and paradise.'

A Somali Bantu refugee, hoping to be resettled in the USA in 2003

Surveys in South-East Asia and the USA show that learning the local language doubles your chance of finding work. In Sweden, refugees are given 240 hours of language classes, free of charge. On the other hand, it is commonly argued that strict limits on migrants and refugees are sensible because it is easier to integrate smaller groups of people.

Resolving conflicts

In many countries, there is great insecurity because of war and persecution. People migrate if they feel threatened, or in desperate circumstances they will flee as refugees. In 2002, Iraqis were the biggest group seeking asylum worldwide. They were trying to escape the brutality of Saddam Hussein's regime, poverty and the threat of US attack. Many are still afraid to return because of the continuing violence in Iraq. What can be done to reduce conflict in the world?

Offering a choice to refugees about their future is important. Most want to return home once the crisis in their country is over. In 2002, some of the one million Sri Lankan refugees headed for their homeland after two decades of civil war. Governments could do more to help returning refugees. But what about those who have settled and made a new life in their host country. They may no longer have strong ties to the country they came from. Should they be allowed to stay?

A new worldwide movement called the World Social Forum works to promote economic

Tamil refugee children on a trailer after returning to Sri Lanka from India in 1995. UNHCR is the United Nations organization that cares for refugees.

and social justice for all. A central belief is that countries should be open to migrants and refugees and offer them equal rights. Maybe some of the movement's ideas for the humane treatment of immigrants and refugees could prove useful?

People being sworn in as citizens in Atlanta, Georgia, USA, at a ceremony performed by the US Immigration and Naturalization Service.

What can we do?

How can individuals be involved? First, they can find out the facts about immigrants and refugees (see page 47 for helpful organizations). Why not try to learn about the different communities in your area, or research your own family background? You might find some surprises! For example, Jacqueline from the UK never felt any connection with Africa until she discovered that her ancestors were Africans taken as

PERSPECTIVES

'If you all had the same religion or something, then it would be so boring. At school you can play with all sorts of friends and find out about different things.'

Maha, aged 12, London

slaves to Jamaica. When she found out about the terrible conditions the slaves had to endure, she felt a new sympathy and closeness with African people.

If there are young people from different backgrounds in your neighbourhood, it is easier to find out about different cultures. Sometimes local groups set up meetings and invite speakers from different communities. For instance, Holocaust Memorial Day, in April in the USA and January in the UK, is a good opportunity to reflect on the plight of refugees during the Second World War and today.

Perhaps there is a youth club or local community group that organizes joint activities for local people and newcomers. In Vermont, USA, for example, World Refugee Day in 2003 was marked with a refugee community picnic to honour the contribution of refugees to the state. At the time, the people of Vermont were preparing to welcome a group of Somali Bantu refugees.

Racism against immigrants and refugees is a serious issue, and it is up to every one of us to tackle it. If you hear racist jokes or see bullying, speak out! Talk to sympathetic kids, teachers and parents. Teachers and students can work together to develop policies to combat racism.

A cultural mix

All countries have a mix of cultures. Newcomers bring their food, music, dance, clothes – and life becomes more varied and interesting for everybody. Immigrants and refugees make an enormous contribution to the culture of their host countries. A few, such as world-class heart-transplant surgeon, Sir Magdi Yacoub, are well known. But we rarely hear about the majority, which includes Esther, a Zimbabwean nurse in London, Felipe, a strawberry picker in California, and Jamila, who runs refugee schools in Pakistan. They work long hours for low pay, contributing to the economy and society. Educating people about the positive aspects of immigration can help to break down barriers, reduce conflict and enable us all to live in a happier environment.

DEBATE

If you are a refugee or new immigrant, how could things be made easier for you? If not, imagine that you were, and how you would like to be welcomed.

Glossary

anti-Semitism hatred of Jewish people.

asylum protection given to people who have left their country because they were in danger.

asylum seeker a refugee who claims the right to live in safety in another country because of persecution in his or her own land.

citizen someone who has a legal right to belong to a particular country.

civil war a war between different groups of people within the same country.

Cold War the hostile relationship between the Western powers and the countries allied to the Soviet Union between 1949 and 1990.

colony land that is ruled by another country.

Communism the system of government in the former Soviet Union (USSR), in which the government controls the production of goods and running of services.

concentration camp a prison where political prisoners are kept in very harsh conditions.

convict someone who has been found guilty of a crime and sent to prison.

detention centre a secure place, like a prison.

developed countries the richer countries of the world, such as those of Europe and North America, which have many industries and a complex economic system.

developing countries the poorer countries of the world, including most of those in Africa, Asia and Latin America, which are working to develop their industries and economic system.

displaced forced to leave home and move to another part of the country.

economic migrant a term for someone who moves to another country to make a better living. Often used negatively.

genocide the deliberate killing of as many people as possible from a particular group.

globalization the development of the free operation of businesses all over the world, permitting them to invest where they want, and employ workers wherever they want.

Gross Domestic Product (GDP) the total value of all the goods and services produced by a country in one year.

Hispanic from a Latin American country.

Holocaust Memorial Day a day to remember the horrors of the Holocaust, held every year.

host country a country that receives refugees.

Internally Displaced Person someone who has been forced to leave his or her home and move to a different part of the country.

integrate to make people members of society.

persecution treating people badly, often because of their ethnic group, culture, religious or political beliefs.

quota the number of immigrants or refugees that can legally enter a country.

trafficker a criminal who generally deceives people into leaving their own countries.

undocumented migrant the correct term for an illegal immigrant.

United Nations an association of most countries in the world that aims to improve social conditions and to solve political problems peacefully.

USSR (the former) Union of Soviet Socialist Republics.

visa a mark or stamp in a person's passport, made by officials of a foreign country, allowing that person to enter or leave.

World Social Forum a worldwide movement for peace, equal rights and social justice.

Useful Addresses

INTERNATIONAL

www.iom.int
International Organization for Migration

www.unhcr.ch
United Nations High Commissioner for Refugees (UNHCR)

USA

www.nnirr.org
National Network for Immigrant and Refugee Rights

www.refugees.org
US Committee for Refugees

UK

www.amnesty.org
Amnesty International

www.exileimages.co.uk
Exile Images
A photo library devoted to photos of refugees and development worldwide, with photo case stories.

www.jcwi.org.uk
Joint Council for the Welfare of Immigrants

www.minorityrights.org
Minority Rights Group International

www.refugeecouncil.org.uk
Refugee Council

www.rsc.ox.ac.uk
Refugee Studies Centre

AUSTRALIA AND NEW ZEALAND

www.refugeecouncil.org.au
Refugee Council of Australia

www.rms.org.nz
Refugee and Migrant Service (New Zealand)

Further Reading

Non-fiction:

Immigration and Asylum: In the News
Iris Teichmann
(Oxford Educational, 2002)

One Day We Had to Run
Sybella Wilkes
(Evans, 2000)

Refugee
Angela Neustatter
(Franklin Watts, 2002)

The State of the World's Refugees
Mark Cutts (ed)
(UNHCR, Oxford University Press, 2000)
Can also be downloaded from the website:
www.unhcr.ch/pubs/sowr2000/sowr2000toc.htm

Why are people refugees?
Cath Senker
(Hodder Wayland, 2004)

World Issues: Refugees
Clive Gifford
(Belitha Press, 2002)

Fiction:

The Other Side of Truth
Beverley Naidoo
(Puffin Books, 2000)

Refugee Boy
Benjamin Zephaniah
(Bloomsbury, 2001)

Teachers' resources:

Credit to the Nation
(Refugee Council, UK, 2002)

Refugees: We left because we had to
(Refugee Council, UK, 2003)

Index

Numbers in **bold** refer to pictures.